The Ten Seduction Secrets of Casanova

Pickup Artists Anonymous

Copyright 2009 – Pickup Artists Anonymous

All rights reserved. No part of this book may be reproduced in any form or by any electronic or mechanical means including information storage and retrieval systems, without permission in writing from the author.

Pickup Artists Anonymous

Pickup Artists (PUA) Anonymous is a fellowship of men who are committed to studying and applying the art of pickup and seduction of women in order to maximise fulfilment of their sexual desires.

Disclaimer:

This book offers suggestions only. The authors / publisher is not responsible for inappropriate use of the information by the reader.

Contents

Chapter 1: What is Seduction? - Page 5

Chapter 2: Who was Giacomo Casanova? - Page 8

Chapter 3: Learning from the Master Seducer - Page 11

Chapter 4: Patterns of Seduction - Page 14

Chapter 5: Mind of Casanova - Page 19

Chapter 6: Ten Seduction Secrets of Casanova - Page 20

Chapter 7: Playing the Role of Casanova - Page 36

Chapter 8: Developing the Casanova Personality - Pg 39

Chapter 9: Developing the Game - Page 69

Chapter 10: Casanova Technique - Page 73

Chapter 11: Seduction Advice - Page 77

Chapter 12: Making the first move - Page 82

Chapter 13: Love making secrets of Casanova - Page 85

Chapter 14: The Casanova Complex - Page 105

Conclusion - Page 108

Casanova Quotes - Page 112

Chapter 1
What is seduction ?

Why is it that Casanova remains such a fascinating figure more than two hundred years after his death?

Surely we must admit it is his legendary sexual appetite. And the fact that he was a man who loved, respected, and appreciated women (and they him). So how does he fare in today's post - Sex and the City world? Let us take a few lessons collected from his experiences as a seducer and recounted in his influential —and hilariously entertaining—memoir, "The Story of My Life"

Benefits of this book

In this book we will teach the Ten Seduction Secrets of Casanova. To gain a better understanding of this man's genius (without reading all 12 volumes of his autobiography), we have summarised the essential ten steps which were used by him in his amorous adventures over and over again.

What is Seduction?

Seduction is the fine art of manipulating people based on physical attraction and desire. It is the act of winning the love or sexual favour of someone. The word seduction stems from Latin and means literally "to lead astray." Seduction is a psychological process by which you can deliberately entice a person to engage in some sort of sexual behaviour. As a result, the term may have a positive or negative connotation.

Seduction, seen negatively, involves temptation and enticement, often sexual in nature, to lead someone astray into a behavioural choice they would not have made if they were not in a state of sexual arousal. Seen positively, seduction is a synonym for the act of charming someone — male or female — by an appeal to the senses, often with the goal of reducing unfounded fear or resistance and leading to their (sexual) emancipation. The seducing agent may even be non-human, such as music or food.

Chapter 2
Who was Casanova ?

Giacomo Girolamo Casanova de Seingalt (April 2, 1725 – June 4, 1798) was a Venetian adventurer and author. His main book 'Histoire de ma vie' (Story of My Life), part autobiography and part memoir, is regarded as one of the most authentic sources of the customs and norms of European social life during the eighteenth century.

Giacomo Casanova was one of history's most famous seducers. The name of Casanova has long been synonymous with seduction, yet the notorious Venetian lived many lives. Priest; lawyer; soldier; scholar; poet; gambler; violinist; lottery director (for King Louis XV of France); Freemason; spy; acquaintance of Voltaire, Rousseau, and Catherine the Great; prisoner (and daring escapee) of the Inquisition -- Giacomo Casanova was all these things and more, but it was his legendary prowess as a seducer of women that got him into Webster's dictionary.

He was so famous as a womaniser that he is sometimes called "the world's greatest lover". He associated with European royalty, popes and cardinals, along with men such as Voltaire, Goethe and Mozart; but if he had not been obliged to spend some years as a librarian in the household of Count Waldstein of Bohemia (where he relieved his boredom by writing the story of his life), it is possible that he would be forgotten today.

During his 73 years, he had seduced and made love to noblewomen, actresses, dancers, chambermaids, Greek slave girls, a priest's niece, a farmer's daughter, five sisters (plus their mother), a transvestite, a hunchback (with "an excitingly misplaced vulva"), a nymphomaniac, and two unrepentant nuns -- 132 ladies in all. He was, quite simply, irresistible. And the 200-odd years that have passed since his death have only embellished his reputation.

Every man, at one time or another, wants to be a Giacomo Casanova.

Chapter 3
Learning from the Master Seducer

Of all history, only one man truly stand out as the Master in the Art of Seduction – Giacomo Casanova.

Many men often have seduction in their minds when they think they have found the right woman. It is therefore no small disappointment when they are thrown the oft quoted cliché. "Let's just be friends." More often than not, this is a female's way of saying, "I don't want to have sex with you at all," or "You stink." What went wrong?

The truth about the art of seduction is that not many people are born with a natural talent for it. On the other hand, some may be born with a natural potential for it but have never been able to exploit the said potential. Just like other forms of art therefore, seducers need to learn the art of seduction from real masters who know what they're doing. There is no better way than to look into the annals of history for one of the greatest seducers of all time – Casanova.

The ability to entice a woman, to get her to surrender what Casanova called her "delicious little that," depends mostly on style and sincerity. That's all there is to it. Although some people may object to Casanova's morals (he revelled in orgies, abhorred condoms, and once made love to his illegitimate daughter), he was not reprehensible.

Casanova wasn't a sexual predator, he was very much in love with most of these women, and they with him. He frequently mentions the multiple orgasms he gave them.

This is certainly flattering, but the fact that he even thought about their pleasure makes him different and admirable.

Casanova was not an aristocrat. He was actually just an ordinary 18th century adventurer but what set him apart was that he was able to practise the art of seduction on 132 women.

He was a man who is amorously and gallantly attentive to women, a promiscuous man, a philanderer. He enjoyed projecting the image of an aristocrat. So while in front of women he appeared highly sophisticated, don't forget that Casanova was, at heart, a philandering rogue who placed fun (sex) and love above all else.

Chapter 4
Patterns of Seduction

In this chapter we will explore the pattern of seduction followed by Casanova. We will try to understand what made him successful.

Casanova was undeniably the only resounding name in the history of the art of seduction. So what was his secret ? What is Casanova trying to tell us about the art of seduction through his memoirs?

For Casanova, as well as his contemporary sybarites of the upper class, love and sex tended to be casual and not endowed with the seriousness characteristic of the Romanticism of the 19th century. Flirtations, bedroom games, and short-term liaisons were common among nobles who married for social connections rather than love. For Casanova, it was an open field of sexual opportunities.

Although multi-faceted and complex, Casanova's personality was dominated by his sensual urges. He wrote "Cultivating whatever gave pleasure to my senses was always the chief business of my life; I never found any occupation more important. Feeling that I was born for the sex opposite of mine, I have always loved it and done all that I could to make myself loved by it."

Casanova's ideal liaison had elements beyond sex, including complicated plots, heroes and villains, and gallant outcomes.

In a pattern he often repeated, he would discover an attractive woman in trouble with a brutish or jealous lover (Stage I); he would ameliorate her difficulty (Stage II); she would show her gratitude; he would seduce her; a short exciting affair would ensue (Stage III); feeling a loss of ardour or boredom setting in, he would plead his unworthiness and arrange for her marriage or pairing with a worthy man, then exit the scene (Stage IV).

Let us look at Casanova's views on seduction. Casanova advises, "There is no honest woman with an uncorrupted heart whom a man is not sure of conquering by dint of gratitude. It is one of the surest and shortest means."

Alcohol and violence, for him, were not proper tools of seduction. Instead, attentiveness and small favours should be employed to soften a woman's heart, but "a man who makes known his love by words is a fool". Verbal communication is essential—"without speech, the pleasure of love is diminished by at least two-thirds"—but words of love must be implied, not boldly proclaimed.

Mutual consent is important, according to Casanova, but

he avoided easy conquests or overly difficult situations as not suitable for his purposes. He strove to be the ideal escort in the first stage—witty, charming, confidential, helpful—before moving into the bedroom in the third stage. Casanova claims not to be predatory. He writes, "my guiding principle has been never to direct my attack against novices or those whose prejudices were likely to prove an obstacle". However, his conquests did tend to be insecure or emotionally exposed women.

The secret of Casanova's success with women had nothing more esoteric in it than offering what every woman who respects herself must demand: all that he had, all that he was, with (to set off the lack of legality) the dazzling attraction of the lump sum money over what is more regularly doled out in a lifetime of instalments.

Casanova valued intelligence in a woman: "After all, a beautiful woman without a mind of her own leaves her lover with no resource after he had physically enjoyed her charms." His attitude towards educated women, however, was typical for his time: "In a woman learning is out of place; it compromises the essential qualities of her sex ... no scientific discoveries have been made by women ... (which) requires a vigour which the female sex cannot have. But in simple reasoning and in delicacy of feeling we must yield to women."

Chapter 5
Mind of Casanova

The manner of Casanova's affairs suggest that he was busy avoiding pain as much as pursuing pleasure; he behaved, more like a man flying from something that he dreads, to the thing he loved.

He would become emotionally attached and then sharply detach himself: his need to leave was as strong as his need to love. What is striking is how repetitive his affairs were, as though he were performing the same scene again and again. At one point, years after a liaison with a nun he calls by the pseudonym MM, he meets another nun and he calls her MM too.

Chapter 6
Ten Seduction Secrets
of Casanova

Casanova understood why some men have an extreme success with women. What Would Casanova Do? In order to understand his Seduction Secrets let us look at these ten secrets from the master's 12 volumes of memoirs.

The legendary lover would apply his 10 principles of sex and seduction and make any woman quiver in her bodice. Just follow along and you can also become a Casanova. The results will be delicious.

Casanova's Secret #1

*To make a woman feel special,
do something special.*

For one of his illicit dinner with 'the good sister', Casanova rented an elegant five-room apartment. He met her as she stepped off the gondola, and they walked arm-in-arm across a lantern-lit plaza.

Your move: When you're trying to impress a woman, never utter these words at the beginning of an evening: "So, what do you feel like doing?" A true Casanova takes charge. He has a plan. To devise a memorable one, imagine that you're proposing. What would you do to make the night so special she couldn't possibly say no? Then arrange it (minus the ring and bent-knee thing, of course). In order to seduce a woman, as the old conqueror was saying, imagine that you must ask her to be your wife and organise the evening as you think best (except for the ring). After all, you are proposing--only it's something far more enticing than marriage. Women are very appreciative of any kind of effort, Casanova certainly realised that.

When you want to impress a woman, do not ever say: "So ... what do you want to do now?" A real Casanova has always a plan; he doesn't hesitate and knows what the next step is. In this way, the woman gains trust in him and lets herself be dominated with pleasure.

Casanova's Secret #2
Privacy is sexy.

In one of his amorous adventures he invites 'the nun' to his house. The nun had a reputation to protect, and Casanova was sensitive to that. The apartment staff did not disturb Casanova and his guest; dinner was served through a window in the wall, allowing the servants to deliver the food without being seen or heard. There were no prying eyes to fear, nothing to distract the two lovers from each other. Privacy gives a woman permission to be herself.

Your move: Create an intimate atmosphere whenever you can. Invite her to dinner at your place, reserve a cosy table at a fine restaurant, encourage her to slip away from the party for a starlit stroll....Continually be searching for eddies in the evening where you both can linger and connect. You can bestow no greater compliment on a woman than your full attention.

A flattered woman is almost conquered. And nothing flatters more a woman than the moment she feels that she has captured the entire attention of a man. If you invite her out, there's no sense to share the evening with other friends. Go with her somewhere away from the noise, from other couples, from everything that could distract her attention. A woman is herself only in privacy.

Casanova's Secret #3

Let her admire you admiring her.

Let her feel fascinated by the fact that...you're fascinated by her.

For most of his amorous adventures, we find that Casanova's rented apartments were full of mirrors and candles. He wanted his love to be "reflected a thousand times," and he wanted to be able to enjoy her from many different angles during dinner. He knew, too, that a beautiful woman enjoys looking at herself--that the mirrors would become her portraits, and she'd feel even sexier because of it. There's a magical quality to mirrors, candlelight, and silver. Women find it enchanting.

Your move: Casanova was inviting women in rooms full of light and mirrors so that they enjoy their image from all angles possible. Also, a woman feels sexier when she looks in a mirror. If you can't duplicate an atmosphere like this, become a mirror yourself. Let her see the effects of her beauty and charm reflected in you. Every now and then, look at her appreciatively and smile. At opportune times, compliment her--choosing a trait other than the obvious. For instance, pretty women are used to being told they're pretty. That kind of compliment has little effect. But tell a pretty woman that she's smart, and you often win her heart. There's a magical quality to a man's open, insightful admiration that women find equally enchanting. Show her what her effect on you is. Smile at her, pay attention to her and don't ask questions to her. Make her think that you can't hear her because of your fascination with her.

Casanova's Secret #4

Ask her what she is thinking about.

Casanova's seduction often lasted several hours, and he spent much of this time asking questions and listening. Such behaviour was flattering to the women. He treated all his female guests respectfully. To Casanova, his women were his equal, and he was genuinely interested in their perspective.

Your move: The reason women found Casanova so fascinating is that he found them so fascinating. In fact, he believed that without engaging conversation, physical pleasure was uninteresting. The minute one starts thinking of the woman as an object, the instant he becomes more interested in himself than in finding out about her. Then you're not being a Casanova. He made women feel valued for things other than their bodies.

It's not difficult to get a woman to talk about herself. Just ask open-ended questions and listen quietly. But you have to be sincere about it. Casanova's success with women stemmed from his genuine interest in them. He touched their hearts before daring to venture any place else.

Show her that your interest for her is deeper than the appearance. That she is not just an ornament. When you perceive a woman as a simple object, you have the tendency to focus more on yourself and then you're not a Casanova. Seducing a woman took many hours for Casanova, time in which he tried to understand them – he knew what to ask and how to listen.

Casanova's Secret #5
Encourage decadence.

For this particular evening, Casanova spared no expense. The apartment, the dinner table, his own body were all dressed with the finest things available. The meal consisted of eight courses, served in pairs. Many of the dishes, such as oysters, champagne, game, sturgeon, truffles, fruits, and sorbets, were delicacies, considered highly indulgent separately, let alone combined with everything else. Casanova was obviously out to impress, but he also knew that after the first sampling of something sinful, it becomes much easier to sin again.

Your move: Provide your lady with something decadent. This could be a single chocolate truffle (gift-wrapped) or an ice-cream sundae that the two of you share. Indulgence is the removal of a single brick that significantly weakens the temple.

If she accepted to go out with you, don't count your pennies in front of her. Exaggerate with your attention. These exaggerations consist in small, but important details: caviar, an expensive present at the first date, the most expensive champagne from the menu. Once she accepted them, she will accept the others (from the bedroom).

Casanova's Secret #6

Appeal to all her senses.

Pay attention to the 5 senses of the woman next to you. Each of them has a small engine that you have to warm.

Casanova scented the apartment with tuberoses because he believed they were an aphrodisiac. He served oysters and champagne as an appetiser because on the tongue there is only one thing more titillating. He asked for his lady's opinions because every woman loves the music of her own voice. He created an atmosphere of lavishness and luxury, so her own indulgence would feel less guilty. And he touched her, often and gently, to return her attention to the true focus of the evening. By stimulating every sense, Casanova was able to immerse this woman more fully in the moment, and make her feel more alive and sexual.

Your move: Be attentive to every one of your lady's five senses. Play background music, touch the small of her back to guide her, make eye contact, give her a flute of champagne to sip, buy her a fresh flower to sniff....

Casanova was using aphrodisiacs. He was perfuming the room with tuberose because it was believed that this flower stimulates the sexual appetite and he was also serving oysters and champagne. He was making her talk- don't forget that any woman enjoys the music of her own voice- and, from time to time, he was touching her slightly to remember her of his presence...

Casanova's Secret #7
Savour the anticipation.

Although Casanova immediately grew "ardent" when he noticed that his lady's breasts were covered by only a dainty chemise, he didn't force himself upon her. He was patient. He accepted her single kiss and cherished her two-word promise: "After supper."

Casanova appreciated that if you have your pleasure too quickly, you don't suck all the pleasure out of it. Savor the anticipation, because often the anticipation is half the fun. Learn to be patient!

Your move: Foreplay doesn't happen only in the bedroom 60 seconds before intercourse. It's organic. It encompasses the entire day. Slip a note into her purse confessing how much you're looking forward to this date, or call her at work and tell her the same. When you meet, take her hands and softly kiss her lips. Most important: Allow the evening to progress at its own pace, remembering that neither of you has to be anywhere except together.

Casanova always thought that if you taste the pleasure too soon, you can't taste it entirely. Remember foreplay begins from the first moment of the date.

Casanova's Secret #8
Be playful.

Most of the food and drink Casanova preferred was sexually suggestive. Plump oysters, succulent game hens, soft cheeses, ripe fruit...on one level, he simply enjoyed watching women put these things in their mouths. But on another, he saw dinnertime as an opportunity for playfulness. When a slippery oyster fell onto an ample bosom, he immediately offered to slurp it off. When the salad arrived undressed, he encouraged the lady to dribble on the oil and vinegar. Casanova realised that sex isn't serious--it's playtime for adults. Games like this are the warm up.

Your move: Whether you're dining at home or at a restaurant, choose something provocative the two of you can share. Put the plate between you and nibble. Eat with your fingers. Feed each other, drink from the same glass. Make it your goal to keep the evening light-hearted.

Casanova's Secret #9
Be spontaneous.

Casanova was an opportunist. He drifted from country to country, working at ludicrously diverse jobs (among them, priest and pimp). He was a disciple of the moment. Once, while sharing a carriage with a farmer's wife during a severe storm, he found her perched on his lap after a frightening thunderclap. Seizing the opportunity, he deftly rearranged her skirts.

Your move: If the evening isn't going according to plan, abandon it. Be attuned to fate and go where it directs. The confidence and daring this shows is in itself seductive.

Casanova was patient, but he wasn't loosing any occasion. When a woman offers herself to you, forget about all the other Commandments and enjoy your luck.

Casanova's Secret #10
Surprise her with sexy gifts.

After supper, Casanova and his lady retired to a candlelit alcove, where he presented her with a beautiful lace nightcap. She pronounced it "magnificent." It was the final, thoughtful coup de grace. "She told me to go undress in the next room," writes Casanova, "promising to call me as soon as she was in bed. This took but two minutes."

Your move: Women love unexpected gifts. Make hers personal rather than trendy, small rather than large, silly rather than serious--something only she can appreciate.

"Casanova's gifts showed a great deal of creativity and thoughtfulness," says Emery. Most important, time your gift's delivery for that critical point in the evening when there remains just one obvious way for her to show her gratitude.

Casanova was buying to women sexy underwear, giving them a reason to try them. Thus, the game was starting. Don't offer to a woman very serious presents from the start: books, fur coats. It's enough to give her something ethereal, a silk scarf, a sexy bodysuit. Ask her to try the outfit in the bathroom and let her make a fascinating presentation. She will already be excited.

Chapter 7
Playing the Role of Casanova

Looking Good Feeling Great

Crucial in the art of seduction is the rule to look good and feel great at the same time. It is surprising to note that the great master of the art of seduction, Casanova was not really the extremely attractive man that he was reported to be. This practitioner of the art of seduction may have had his charms but he was no Movie Star. He did however, take care of his body. This is not to say though that modern male students of the art of seduction should be too physically conscious. It is perhaps enough that you keep proper hygiene, have properly pressed clothes, and well-combed hair.

Alpha State

It is also important in the art of seduction to follow the footsteps of the alpha male, Casanova. At the age of eighteen, this true master of the art of seduction became a doctor of law. Although he led a modest career, he was intelligent and mentally quick. In modern times, he may not all be able to have doctoral degrees, but the point here is that women love men who have their acts together and who actually have something to show for themselves. The art of seduction is all about being the alpha male. It can be even something like some specific goal in life, something which shows you are different from the rest.

Subtlety

The great master of the art of seduction also wants to tell us that seduction is not just about outright aggression.

Seduction should be a subtle process like Casanova initiating some gentle pre-sex talk.

The great master of the art of seduction is trying to teach us to be confident, be achievers and be subtle in your approach.

Chapter 8
Developing the Casanova personality

Casanova: the greatest lover, a man who was a promiscuous and unscrupulous lover. "Unscrupulous," it turns out, is something of a bum rap. Our man Giacomo Casanova was a strict practitioner of the Golden Rule where his romantic conquests were concerned. Casanova was a libertine but he was no cad. "Never to harm a mistress, never to arouse her anger or disappointment, never to make her suffer from their affair in any way -- this is what he consistently aspires to," writes the Belgian psychoanalyst Lydia Flem.

The pay-off was that Casanova's women loved him back. As Flem notes, "Giacomo showers his lovers with discreet care, kind attentions, elegant gifts, joyful surprises, and in his memoirs he respectfully gives the best-known among them anonymity. Generous, indeed prodigal, he gives without counting; he gives more than he owns. He likes to cause surprise, wonder, and happiness ... . He will do anything to fulfil a woman's expectations, certain of making her pleased with him if he can make her pleased with herself. This is perhaps the most reliable way he has found of obtaining a lady's favours."

1) Be an opportunist

"The lover who is not ready to take Fortune by the forelock is lost," writes Casanova. This was a man who claimed opportunism as his motto and who consistently seized every willing woman whom chance threw his way. That meant hundreds of them. Wherever he lodged in his frequent travels, Casanova's hosts always seemed to have a teen-aged daughter or servant girl (or two) ripe for the plucking. Actresses, nuns, other men's wives -- fortune brought beauties of all kinds to Casanova, and he generally found a way to bed them.

When he couldn't literally get them into bed, shared carriage rides proved as much opportunities for seducing married women as they were a form of transportation.

Casanova first has sex with Donna Lucrezia Castelli, for instance, while they are riding in a carriage. Then there is the young bride he meets on a trip to Pasiano. This woman's oafish husband is rudely ignoring her and flirting with her prettier sister, and Casanova suggests that she give the husband something to be jealous of himself. She agrees to play along, but she does so unconvincingly, and when Casanova presses her to make the infidelity real, she refuses to do anything so abominable with a priest (our hero, still a teenager, hadn't yet been drummed out of the seminary). Casanova makes no further headway with her until they share a carriage ride during a fierce sudden storm:

"There is a flash of lightning, then another, thunder rumbles, and the poor woman is shaking all over. The rain comes down. I take off my cloak to use it to cover us both in front; and, heralded by an enormous flash, the lightning strikes a hundred paces ahead. The horses rear, and the poor lady is seized by spasmodic convulsions. She throws herself on me and clasps me in her arms. I bend forward to pick up the cloak, which had fallen to our feet, and, as I pick it up, I raise her skirts with it. Just as she is trying to pull them down again, there is another flash of lightning, and her terror deprives her of the power to move. Wanting to put the cloak over her again, I draw her toward me; she literally falls on me, and I quickly put her astride me. Since her position could not be more propitious, I lose no time, I adjust myself to it in an instant by pretending to settle my watch in the belt of my breeches. Realising that if she did not stop me at once, she could no longer defend herself, she makes an effort, but I tell her that if she does not pretend to have fainted, the postilion will turn and see everything. So saying, I leave her to call me an impious monster to her heart's content, I clasp her by the buttocks, and carry off the most complete victory that ever a skilful swordsman won."

2) *Facing life fearlessly (With Certain Exceptions)*

Read a dozen volumes of memoirs and you get to know Casanova. He found that facing up to his misadventures were the surest way to get him out of trouble. "The trick I used to accomplish this," he explains, "was to relate the facts truthfully, not omitting certain circumstances which it takes courage to reveal. Therein lies the secret, which not everyone can apply, for the greater part of the human race is made up of cowards; I know from experience that truth is a talisman whose charms are unfailing, provided that it is not wasted on fools. I believe that a guilty man who dares admit his guilt to a just judge is more likely to be absolved than an innocent man who equivocates."

On the other hand, neither did Casanova claim, as legend says his contemporary George Washington did, an inability to lie. Casanova, in his words, "had no scruples about deceiving nitwits and fools when I found it necessary. As for women, this sort of reciprocal deceit cancels itself out, for when love enters in, both parties are usually dupes."

With women, Casanova was capable of telling preposterously bold lies -- and of having them be believed. None is more outlandish than the one he tells the woman he calls "Miss XCV." This beautiful young woman's lover has gotten her pregnant and skipped town, and her mother is trying to marry her off to an older man she despises. Casanova immediately falls in love with her, but, despite Casanova's approach, she wants only to be friends. Casanova is the only person she confides her pregnancy to, and she asks him, as a trusted friend, to help her obtain an abortion.

Casanova eventually asks an older woman with an interest in alchemy if she knows of any sure method of bringing on an abortion without endangering the pregnant woman. She recommends the use of aroph, a medicine advocated by the 16th-century alchemist Paracelsus.

Casanova describes the procedure thus: "The woman who hoped to empty her womb was to put a dose of this opiate on the end of a cylinder of the proper size and insert it into her vagina in such a way as to stimulate the round piece of flesh at the top of her such-and-such. The cylinder must at the same time stimulate the channel leading to the closed door of the little house which sheltered the little enemy whose departure was sought. This procedure, repeated three or four times a day for six or seven days, so weakened the little door that it finally opened and the foetus tumbled out.

"Laughing heartily at the prescription," he continues, "whose absurdity was instantly apparent to common sense, I gave Madame back her precious manuscript and I spent two hours reading the always astonishing Paracelsus and then Boerhaave, who discusses aroph like a reasonable man."

His finding the procedure ridiculous, however, doesn't prevent Casanova from passing it on to Miss XCV, along with an imaginative twist of his own. "It was on the spur of the moment," he informs us, "that it occurred to me to tell her that the aroph had to be mixed with sperm which had not lost its natural heat for a single instant." That is,

Miss XCV, her lover unavailable, would be required to borrow some friend's penis for use as the cylinder needed to apply the aroph, a loan which the ever-gallant Casanova happily volunteered to make. She eventually, albeit sceptically, agrees. Casanova's play-by-play of the start of their week-long aroph-application regimen follows:

"In our utter seriousness we appeared to be a surgeon getting ready to perform an operation and the patient who submits to it. Miss was the operating surgeon. She sets the open box at her right, then lies down on her back, and, spreading her thighs and raising her knees, arches her body; at the same time, by the light of the candle, which I am holding in my left hand, she puts a little crown of aroph on the head of the being who is to convey it to the orifice where the amalgamation is to be accomplished. The astonishing thing is that we neither laughed nor felt any desire to laugh, so engrossed were we in our roles. After the insertion was completed, the timid Miss blew out the candle, but two minutes later she had to let me light it again. The thing had been done to perfection so far as I was concerned, but she did not feel sure about herself. I obligingly said that I did not mind repeating the performance. My formal tone made us both laugh ... ."

3) *The Importance of being Desirous*

The extravagant praise Casanova always lavished on the objects of his desire feels out-of-place in our own irony-steeped times. But Casanova learned early on that it is impossible to praise a woman too much, and all to easy to squander an opportunity for sex by not praising her enough.

In fact, Casanova lost his own virginity at age 15 in a threesome with two sisters because of all the praise he'd been heaping on a friend of theirs. As he put it, "Not being conceited enough to suppose that the two girls could fall in love with me from listening to my complaints, not only did I not restrain myself in their presence, I confided my troubles to them when Angela was not there. I often spoke to them with an ardour far greater than that with which I addressed the cruel girl who quelled it in me. The genuine lover is always afraid that the object of his love will think he is exaggerating; and fear of saying too much makes him say less than is the case."

Casanova never does bed Angela, but it is not long before he finds himself sleeping between the Savorgnan sisters, at the start of a three-way relationship that would continue off-and-on for several years afterward: "I began with the one toward whom I was turned, not knowing whether it was Nanetta or Marta. I found her curled up and covered by her sheet, but by doing nothing to startle her and proceeding step by step as gradually as possible, I soon convinced her that her best course was to pretend to be asleep and let me go on. Little by little I straightened her out, little by little she uncurled, and little by little, with slow, successive, but wonderfully natural movements, she put herself in a position which was the most favourable she could offer me without betraying herself. I set to work, but to crown my labours it was necessary that she should join in them openly and undeniably, and nature finally forced her to do so."

He then "turned the other way to do the same thing with her sister" but "at the moment of crisis she no longer had the strength to keep up her pretence. Throwing off the mask, she clasped me in her arms and pressed her mouth on mine."

The second conquest, it turns out, is Nanetta, as Casanova discovers when Marta rises from bed and lights a candle.

"When I saw Nanetta in my arms on fire with love, and Marta holding a candle and looking at us, seeming to accuse us of ingratitude for not saying a word to her, when, by having been the first to yield to my caresses, she had encouraged her sister to imitate her, I realised all my good fortune."

"'Let us get up,' I said, 'and swear eternal friendship and then refresh ourselves.'

"Under my direction the three of us made an improvised toilet in a bucket of water, which set us laughing and renewed all our desires; then, in the costume of the Golden Age, we finished the rest of the tongue and emptied the other bottle. After our state of sensual intoxication had made us say a quantity of those things which only love can interpret, we went back to bed and spent the rest of the night in ever varied skirmishes."

4) Way to a woman's heart is through her stomach

As with men, Casanova's memoirs suggest, the way to a woman's heart is through her stomach. Whenever he could possibly afford it, Casanova threw lavish feasts when wooing women. He loved mixing them with rum or champagne punches as part of the seduction. And he especially enjoyed fooling around with woman and oysters.

Here, for instance, is a glimpse of an affair with the gorgeous libertine nun M.M., whom Casanova has fallen for while visiting his previous love, C.C., at the convent she has been exiled to after Casanova got her pregnant: "After making punch we amused ourselves eating oysters, exchanging them when we already had them in our mouths. She offered me hers on her tongue at the same time that I put mine between her lips; there is no more lascivious and voluptuous game between two lovers, it is even comic, but comedy does no harm, for laughter is only for the happy. What a sauce that is which dresses an oyster I suck from the mouth of the woman I love! It is her saliva. The power of love cannot but increase when I crush it, when I swallow it."

Maybe it is something about convents, but many years later Casanova introduces a beautiful teenaged resident of another convent, and the girl's only slightly elder governess, Emilia, to the oyster game. These two young ladies are no libertines, but they both take an immediate liking to oysters. The trio consumes 100 of them their first evening dining together, with a full meal in between the first 50 and the last, and the girls enjoy the oysters so much that the three of them get together for a repeat performance several days afterward. This time, Casanova pushes his luck too far, and suffers a temporary setback: "It was by chance that a fine oyster which I gave Emilia, putting the shell to her lips, dropped into her bosom; she made to recover it; but I claimed that it was mine by right, and she had to yield, let me unlace her, and gather it with my lips from the depth to which it had dropped. In the course of this she had to bear with my uncovering her bosom completely; but I retrieved the oyster in such a way that there was no sign of my having felt any pleasure except that of having recovered, chewed, and swallowed it. Armellina watched the whole procedure without smiling, surprised that I appeared to show no interest in what I must have seen. Four or five oysters later I gave one to Armellina, who was sitting on my lap, and I cleverly dropped it into her bosom, which brought a laugh from Emilia, who at bottom was annoyed that Armellina had escaped a test of an intrepidity such as she had shown me. But I saw that Armellina was delighted by the mishap, though she refused to give any sign of it.

"'I want my oyster,' I said.

"'Take it.'

"I unlace her whole bodice, and, the oyster having dropped down as far as possible, I complain that I shall have to bring it up with my hand. Good God! What torment for a man in love to have to hide the excess of his delight at such a moment! Armellina had not the slightest pretext to accuse me of anything, for I did not touch her beautiful breasts, hard as marble, except in searching for the oyster. After retrieving and swallowing it, I took hold of one of her breasts, demanding the liquid from the oyster which had spilled on it; I seized the rosebud with my avid lips, surrendering to all the voluptuous feelings inspired in me by the imaginary milk which I sucked for a good two or three minutes. I saw that she was surprised and moved; but when I let her go, it was only to recover my soul, which my great pleasure had made to exhale where I did not know if she could suspect it. But when she saw me fix my eyes on hers as if in a stupor, she asked me if I had very much enjoyed imitating the babe at the breast.

"'Yes, for it is an innocent game.'

"'I do not believe so, and I hope you will say nothing about it to our Superioress; what you did is not innocent for me, and we must retrieve no more oysters.'"

5) *Threesome is Company*

Nanetta and Marta, C.C. and M.M., Armellina and Emilia -- threesomes are a recurring theme in Casanova's life, and he makes it clear that this is no accident, while offering parents a counterintuitive tip on how to keep their daughters chaste.

During a stay in Geneva, Casanova manages to turn a theological discussion into a lakeside game of doctor with the cousins Hedwig, 22, and Helena, 16. Three days later, the girls have arranged to sneak a night in bed together with him. As Casanova the lover hides in a closet awaiting their arrival, Casanova the memoirist interrupts his narrative to debunk the effectiveness of chaperones.

"In my long career as a libertine, during which my invincible inclination for the fair sex led me to employ every method of seduction, I turned the heads of several hundred women whose charms had overwhelmed my reason; but what was always my best safeguard is that I was always careful not to attack novices, girls whose moral principles or whose prejudices were an obstacle to success, except in the company of another woman. I early learned that what arouses resistance in a young girl, what makes it difficult to seduce her, is lack of courage; whereas when she is with a female friend she gives in quite easily; the weakness of the one brings about the fall of the other. Fathers and mothers believe the contrary, but they are mistaken. They commonly refuse to entrust their daughter to a young man, whether for a ball or a walk; but they yield if the girl has one of her friends as a chaperon. I repeat for their benefit: they are mistaken; for if the young man knows how to go about it their daughter is lost. A false shame prevents both girls alike from offering an absolute resistance to seduction, and as soon as the first step has been taken the fall comes inevitably and quickly. If the friend permits the theft of the slightest favour in order to save herself from blushing, she will be the first to urge her friend to grant a greater one, and if the seducer is skilful the innocent novice will, without realising it, have gone too far to turn back. Then, too, the more innocent a girl is, the more unacquainted she will be with the methods and the end of seduction. Without her being aware of it, the lure of pleasure draws her on, curiosity enters in, and opportunity does the rest.

6) Keeping all options open

Many guys let practical considerations -- women's boyfriends, geographic distance, and similar nuisances -- block their way to romance. Casanova, renowned in his day for his breakout from the Inquistion's "escape-proof" Leads Prison, would be appalled at such spiritless surrenders. After all, when he met the greatest love of his life, the mysterious Henriette, she was disguised as a boy and traveling illicitly with an Hungarian army officer; rather than back off, Casanova helps the couple out of a jam and sweet-talks the Hungarian into turning Henriette over to him. And it is the oyster-eating nun M.M who first initiates him as a libertine, at a time when, besides being sequestered in a convent, she is already carrying on an affair with a French ambassador.

In his fighting prime, Casanova even managed once to overcome two apparently "impossible" situations almost simultaneously.

First comes the Greek slave girl Casanova spots while under a 28-day quarantine at Ancona. The Greek girl is free to come and go in a garden beneath the balcony outside his room, and they soon contrive a way to raise half her body through a hole in the balcony's floor. During a third such rendezvous, Casanova is on the verge of pulling her up to him in her entirety when a guard comes up behind him, grabs the naked, hunched-over Casanova by the shoulders, and demands to know what is going on. The slave girl flees, Casanova's quarantine ends the next day, and that looks to be the end of that.

A few months later, after trips to Naples and Rome, Casanova returns to Ancona, where he is introduced to the castrato Bellino. "This anomalous being," he writes, "had some of Donna Lucrezia's features and certain gestures reminiscent of the Marchesa G. The face seemed to me feminine and the masculine attire did not prevent my seeing a certain fullness of bosom, which put it into my head that despite the billing, this must be a girl. In this conviction, I made no resistance to the desires which he aroused in me."

Despite much pleading, Bellino refuses Casanova's advances, and Casanova makes due with one-night alliances with the castrato's two sisters. Bellino does, however, ask Casanova to let him travel with him to the town of Rimini, where Bellino is scheduled to sing. He agrees, and the day before they are to depart, Casanova decides to host a dinner party for the Spaniard who had introduced him to Bellino. Casanova takes Bellino with him on a walk to the Ancona port, where he buys a small barrel of oysters for that night's party. Their walk soon takes them to a Turkish vessel making ready to sail for Alexandria.

"Scarcely aboard, the first person I see is the beautiful Greek girl whom I had left in the lazaretto at Ancona seven months earlier. She was beside the old captain. I pretend not to see her and ask him if he has any fine merchandise to sell. He takes us to his cabin and opens his closets. I read in the Greek girl's eyes her joy at seeing me again. Nothing that the Turk showed me having suited me, I told him that I would be glad to buy something pretty, such as might please his fairer half. He laughs, she speaks to him in Turkish, and he goes off. She comes running and throws herself on my neck, and, clasping me to her bosom, says: 'Fortune gives us this one moment.' My courage being no less than hers, I sit down, accommodate her to my position, and in less than a minute do what her master had never done to her in five years. I plucked the fruit, and I was eating it; but to swallow it I needed another minute. The poor Greek girl, hearing her master coming back, left my arms and turned her back to me, thus giving me time to set myself to rights without his seeing my disordered state, which could well have cost me my life, or all the money I possessed, to bring to an amicable settlement. What amused me in this really serious situation was to see Bellino struck motionless by surprise and shaking with fear."

Two days later, after one more failed attempt by Casanova to prove Bellino a woman, the two of them leave for Rimini. Overnighting together at an inn en route, Bellino surprises Casanova by agreeing to share his room. They no sooner get into bed together than they begin a lengthy session of lovemaking, during which Casanova's suspicions about Bellino being a woman are finally vindicated.

7) *Marriage can be the end of passion*

Casanova never did marry, though he did propose marriage several times, including once to Bellino / Teresa. Typically, the proposals were sincere when he was making them, but quickly cast aside once he'd made his conquest, as with the pretty country girl Cristina. Casanova shares a gondola ride with Cristina and her uncle, a priest, who has brought her to Venice on a two-week trip to hunt for a husband. On the ride, Casanova lists the reasons he'd had for rejecting a series of potential wives. One was "intolerably vain," another couldn't give him children, another was "too pious," and others were a know-it-all, gloomy, a prude, had bad breath, and wore make-up. Cristina has none of these faults, and Casanova soon works around to proposing to and seducing her.

"No later than the next day I decided to make Cristina happy without marrying her. I had had the idea when I still loved her more than myself. After I enjoyed her, the scales swung to my side so far that my self-love proved to outweigh the love her charms had inspired in me. I could not bring myself, by marrying, to give up all the hopes which depended on my staying in my state of freedom."

A much less typical proposal is the one the 35-year-old

Casanova makes to a beautiful 17-year-old named Leonilda he meets on a trip to Naples after an absence of 18 years. This one he reneges on immediately when he learns that, well, Leonilda is his daughter -- by Donna Lucrezia Castelli. Casanova doesn't marry Leonilda, but the very night Donna Lucrezia startles him with the news that she is their daughter, the three go to bed together:

"... it was Leonilda who undressed her mother, while, after wrapping my hair in a kerchief, I threw my clothes into the middle of the room. She tells her daughter to get into bed beside her.

"'Your father,' she says, 'will confine his attention to your mother.'

"'And I,' she replies, 'will give mine to you both'; and, on the other side of the bed she undresses completely and gets in next to her, saying that as her father I was at liberty to see all my handiwork. Her mother is proud of her, she praises her, and she rejoices to see that I find her beautiful. It sufficed her that she was in the middle and that it was only upon her that I extinguished the fire with which she saw that I was burning. Leonilda's curiosity delighted me to the soul.

"'So is that what you did,' she asked me, 'when you engendered me eighteen years ago?'

"But the moment which leads Lucrezia to the death of love has come, just when, to spare her, I feel it my duty to withdraw. Moved to pity, Leonilda sends her mother's little soul on its flight with one hand and with the other puts a white handkerchief under her gushing father."

8) *Word of Caution*

Love can be dangerous, and sometimes rules are meant to

be broken. Avoid marriage? Casanova has some second thoughts on that one himself late in life, as when he pauses here to reflect on a favourite old flame: "Madame Lebel is one of the ten or twelve women whom I loved the most fondly in my happy youth. She had everything one could ask to make a happy marriage if it had been my destiny to enjoy that felicity. But with my character I may have done well not to bind myself irrevocably, though at my present age my independence is a sort of slavery. If I had married a woman intelligent enough to guide me, to rule me without my feeling that I was ruled, I should have taken good care of my money, I should have had children, and I should not be, as now I am, alone in the world and possessing nothing."

The only things certain about love, Casanova suggests, are its uncertainty, and that anyone pursuing it must be prepared to take the bad with the good.

"What is love? For all that I have read every word that certain self-styled sages have written concerning its nature, for all that I have philosophised on it myself as I have grown older, I will never admit that it is either a trifle or a vanity of vanities. It is a kind of madness over which philosophy has no power; a sickness to which man is prone at every time of life and which is incurable if it strikes in old age. Inexpressible love! God of nature! Bitterness than which nothing is sweeter; sweetness than which nothing is more bitter! Divine monster which can only be defined by paradoxes!"

Chapter 9
Developing the Game

Developing the Seduction Game. For thousands of years in our human history, the art of seduction of women remained very much a mystery for men in general.

A few "gifted" guys, being naturally blessed with the skill of picking up women, found it very easy to attract and seduce women. On the other hand, other guys had a very hard time getting any dates with girls.

Fortunately these days, the art of seducing women is no longer a mystery and the skill can now be taught to any man alive, even those with ZERO natural talent. And you don't even have to be rich, famous or good looking to become a successful "seducer."

There are three stages to any successful "Seduction Game"

- *Approach:*

Never approach a woman with your body fully facing her. This signals far too much interest and you'll give off a desperate "vibe." Instead, try to stand at a slight angle to her body. Always start the conversation with a comment, question or statement consisting of two qualities: humour and coolness.

- *Building Trust:*

The aim of this stage is to get a woman feeling that she can trust you enough to get physically "intimate" with you. You do this through the art of story-telling. Any story that shows your sensitive human side. For example, how you just lost your dear pet dog Buster, that you've had since you were ten years old. Or how you once helped a stranger while on holiday by protecting them from some local thugs. By telling stories like this, she would feel like she's known you for years even if she only just met you. When you do this correctly, you dramatically speed up the process of having an intimate physical relationship with her. If you don't do this right you could end up having to take her out on countless dates before you even kiss her.

- ***Seduction:***

This is where you "close the deal" so to speak in a pick up situation. Women usually feel "cheap" if they get physical with a guy too soon in a relationship.

So the key to seduction is to use playful "physical" games to distract her from feeling "slutty." This will also give her an excuse to feel okay being touched by you. Palm reading is probably the best thing you can do here. Start by taking her hand in yours and playfully reading it. Then progress to playing other games that involves her elbows, shoulders, lips and other body parts. So learn some games and apply them in your seduction. Just be sure you do it very slowly, don't just jump from the hands to the face. The key to success is to move to each new stage very "gradually." These are just a few of the tips which men can use every day in order to become "modern day Casanova" seducers.

Chapter 10
Casanova Technique

Seduction is not necessarily about having a perfect body, or a perfect personality, or a perfect wealth and social status. There are many that seem to know how to seduce girls, without being the most beautiful, or the most clever, or the richest men. You can, too, do that, if you learn some proper Casanova techniques.

The perfect path to seduce her is through the ears and tongues of others. Be nice with the people around you, and especially with those that you know that come in contact with her. Tell them what you like about her, and that will usually reach her ears, as well.

Being a Casanova is a thing of attitude. When it comes to conversations about sex, do not be blunt about the subject. It will serve well to understand how you can construct the reputation of a subtle man. Read more about the most successful male personalities with a lot of lovers, and see how they expressed their interest about sex. Use hints instead of direct statements, when the subject comes up.

Faking indifference is a cool way to attract even the most gorgeous girl in the crowd. As your reputation is known now, it will not be long until she will ask herself why you do nothing to get to court her.

Women care what other females think. So, if you just send the word that there are others liking you, that will make her be interested in you.

In this stage, the wisest thing to do is to wait for her to make a move. When she begins to get close to you and starts to flirt, now it is the time for a new move. The sound of your voice must be seductive, avoid saying anything about you, talk casually about everything, but never forget to mention sex once in a while, without concentrating too much on it. Your eyes should be glued to her during these conversations.

Usually, guys must pretend to be powerful and confident. Apologising will always be interpreted as a sign of weakness, so avoid showing that. Still, some strategic weakness can be shown with some success, but it will require a great skill in pretending. As girls have a certain fear of men at some level, you will need to show that you are sensitive and you can be hurt too. This does not mean that you should get depressed or conduct a conversation about a subject that really makes you hurt. Just mention a scene in a movie that you are sure that impressed her, and tell her that it had impressed you, too.

Flirting is good, but it will not bring you anything, if you prolong this stage for too much. A girl will show interest in you, more and more, while you are flirting with her, but, if that goes like this for too long, you will end up watching her taking her leave, as she begins to be tired of waiting you to make a move. Balance the moment when it would be best to ask her out and do it.

Finally, she will fall in your lap. Soon, you will be able to get intimate with her, but do not forget about seducing her constantly. Offer her compliments, and move slowly, so she does not get scared. She will end up craving for your touch, and you must show your appreciation for her gift.

Chapter 11
Seduction Advice of Casanova

Don't beat around the bush.

Casanova writes "The very next morning I sent the following note to La Valville: I would like, madame, to have an affair with you. You have awakened distressing desires in me, which I challenge you to satisfy."

Appeal to her rational side.

"She told me it was in my power to seduce her, but that if I loved her, I should spare her this shame. I made it clear to her that an intelligent girl could only be ashamed of giving herself to a man she did not love; but if she loved me, then love, assuming responsibility for everything, would justify her in everything."

Agonise over her.

"After giving her a faithful account of the state in which her charms had put me and the pains I had suffered for having resisted the inclination to give her clear signs of my affection, I told her that, as I could no longer endure the torment her presence caused my enamoured soul, I found myself with no choice but to ask her please not to appear before my eyes any more.... I described to her the frightful consequences that might bring us unhappiness if we were to act otherwise than in the manner her virtue and mine had forced me to propose to her.... We then spent a good hour in the most eloquent silence, broken only by Lucia's crying out from time to time: 'Ah! My God! Is it possible I am not dreaming?'"

Be persistent, if you think
she's the woman for you.

"We sat down to eat; and in his speech, his attitude, the expression in his eyes, and his smiles, Bellino seemed like a different person.... Once in bed, I shuddered as I saw him draw near.... At last we took a rest. An intermission was in order. But we were not exhausted; our senses merely needed for our minds to calm down before they could fall back into place. Bellino was the first to break the silence, asking me if I thought she was a loving mistress. 'Mistress?' I said. 'So you admit you are a woman?'"

Be patient.

"She could see I was burning for her, and as she seemed pleased with my restraint, I asked her if she would mind if I called on her often.... Our intimacy began one evening after supper, when she was overcome by convulsions that lasted the entire night. I did not leave her bedside, and the following day I was justly rewarded for my twenty-six years of constancy."

Praise her experience.

"I finally realised she was afraid I would reproach her if I found she was not a virgin. Her anxiety amused me, and I was pleased to assure her that the virginity of girls seemed to me nothing more than an invention of boys, since nature had deprived most girls of even the signs of it. I ridiculed those who made it a question of honour. I could see that my wisdom pleased her, and she came into my arms full of confidence."

Show your gratitude.

"Each discovery I made raised my soul to love, which in

turn fortified me in the demonstration of my gratitude. She was astonished to find herself receptive to so much pleasure, for I showed her many things she had considered fictions. I did things to her that she did not feel she could ask me to do and I taught her that the slightest constraint spoils the greatest pleasures."

Give as good as you get.

"Cultivating the pleasures of the senses was my principle concern throughout my life; none, indeed, was ever more important to me. Feeling as though I was born for the fair sex, I have always loved it and let it love me as much as I could."

Chapter 12
Making the first move

In order to learn how to seduce a woman you need to understand that the most important thing is to pinpoint the moment when a woman wants to have sex as much as you do. A woman wants to be pursued and desired by a man. You must have enough courage to make the first move. Once you make the first move you are on the path of knowing how to seduce a woman.

When you decide to make the first move it is important to understand that it is only natural to be nervous. The best time to make a first move is during a transitional stage in a relationship. This is when a relationship goes from being non physical to physical. You want to locate opportunities where you can move ahead and interact with a woman.

The transition should be well planned in order to seduce the woman. When figuring out how to seduce a woman you must always plan ahead like Casanova did in most cases. You should jot down certain moments such as where you can progress from getting a woman's number, to touching her, to kissing her and to seducing her. The transition should seem non-offensive and non-intentional. You do not want to come on as being too aggressive or too needy.

When you are learning how to seduce a woman you should understand a woman from deep within. This means that you must understand what she wants in order for you to progress. She may want a man who is confident or a man who is a gentleman or a man who is interested in a specific cause. Find out what she responds to, in order to be successful.

When you are making the first move remember to be methodical, articulate and calculative. Plan ahead and know how to seduce a woman. You should set the scene so to speak. Seducing a woman is an art form that has a certain rhythm. The progression from friends to intimacy should be well thought out and smooth.

Make a woman desire you. Seduction is a two way street. When you make the first move make sure that the woman is responding to your filtrations. Evaluate her smile and gestures. These will allow you to know when the perfect moment has arrived to practice the art of seduction. As many seduction experts agree even a player or Casanova must be smooth and articulate when seducing a woman. This is how Casanova seduced women after women.

Chapter 13
Love-making Secrets of Casanova

Giacomo Casanova is perhaps one of the most famous "lovers" of all time. By his own accounts, he had in his life 132 affairs, and they were all special events. Casanova had some secret love techniques.

When Casanova was arrested by the Inquisition, they found among his papers and books a volume of Aretino's book on sexual positions.

This is a unique dialogue between two women that had both been wife, prostitute and nun. They describe their favourite positions and techniques, which no doubt, Casanova made very good use of.

Casanova's sexual techniques, and secrets, were not at all limited to the bedroom. Reading though his autobiography we find a general pattern of activity that contributed to his success with women.

His secret love techniques began the moment he met the woman. The routine he followed was flawless in its execution and planning, and was always a success.

- ***Study the woman. How is she dressed? How has she presented herself to the world?***

- ***Decide on some small gift.***

In Casanova's days, chocolate (as a drink) was novel and expensive. He would prepare it for the lady himself, personally. Some other women he would present flowers, or an expensive bonnet (very fashionable then), or some trinket of beautify. Think this doesn't work, think again.

- *Arrange for a meal.*

It was difficult for Casanova to divorce the pleasures of the table with those of the bedroom. He would always feed his lovers, in advance of any other activity if he had the chance.

- *Be forward and dominant.*

Casanova was always the man that took the lead. In his concept, women prefer men of this category, and his life showed this to be true.

The above technique brought Casanova to the point where he could employ the positions mentioned in Aretino's Dialogue.

Casanova had his absolute favourites, to be exact. Side to Side, with woman's leg raised. In this position, Casanova reclines holding his head up with one arm, and the raised leg of the woman with the other. He would penetrate from the rear, but underneath, and forceful thrusting. This position is for the normal to large sized man, and is super pleaser to the woman. Although there is no clitoral stimulation, there is direct G-spot and AFE Zone (Anterior Fornix Erogenous Zone) stimulation.

The second position was by far Casanova's favourite, and was used with those women he wished to express his love for.

Casanova would sit on the edge of a bed with his legs on the floor. He would mount the woman on top of him, with her legs wrapped around his waste, her arms around his neck. There is no thrusting. The woman would be penetrated in this pose to gain maximum clitoral stimulation and G-spot/AFE Zone all at the same time. The woman would be pressed to the maximum penetration, and he would move in circles and then a rocking motion.

As the world's greatest lover, Casanova employed this techniques again and again because they worked and worked well.

Do not forget the preliminaries and foreplay. All we read about in foreplay was copious amounts of kissing, but we can let our own imagination tell us what the Master Lover was doing.

His greatest secret in love however, was revealed in one comment, which is "Real love is the love that sometimes arises after sensual pleasure: if it does, it is immortal; the other kind inevitably goes stale, for it lies in mere fantasy."

Men, you can learn from Casanova and in this way his legacy lives on!

Foreplay

It is highly doubtful that many people today have read the whole autobiography of Casanova's life. It is after all, literature, and not in any sense pornography. However a careful read though gives one the feeling of the 18th Century in Europe (as Casanova travelled in many countries). His sexual conduct was limited to only 167 romantic conquests. He was, however, a master of seduction, and his techniques of foreplay, as appropriate today as it was over 200 years ago.

Casanova would measure the courses, and the meal to match his conversation and stories. He would spark the lady's imagination with stories from his esoteric repertoire and even indicate to them their fortunes. His concept was to break down any conditioned responses to rejecting his advances. So, keeping the stomach full, the head light, and the mind occupied did the trick. All this during the meal itself. Casanova would take the meal across from the lady, but slowly he would sit closer, and by the dessert, he and the lady were in very close company.

Planning

To say that Casanova was spontaneous in his approach to bedding women would be a mistake. He was a careful planner, something akin to a general to an impending battle. He would do research on the target (meaning he was a proto-psychologist), and also, carefully think ahead of ways to achieve his desired result. Most of his plans were clever, and very entertaining to read about.

Pleasing His Partner

Being Italian, and of the great city Venice, Casanova was a master of many of the personal arts, one among them was cooking. In a tavern or home, he was very careful to either prepare his meals himself, or to supervise their preparation. He had a few standard "pleasers" for his women, as he knew they were sure to please. They were:

- Hot or cold chocolate drink. Remember, chocolate and coffee were still novel at that time
- Shell fish, especially the oyster. He was the first to write about its aphrodisiac qualities
- Sparkling wine and fruit (one might imagine strawberries).
- Always a desert with a variety of sweets presented

You can see from the list above, Casanova was ingenious in the use of foods as a tool for seduction. Meals during that period were not delicate, but heavy with stews and soups. Casanova would prepare (or have prepared) meals of utmost delicacy and spare no expense. His only idea was to please his partner but catering to their basic desires, eating being one of them

Closing Techniques

Closing was his greatest talent. He knew the value of foreplay, and employed it in all its aspects. The final form of finally kissing and fondling his prospective partner came after much teasing and implication. Casanova was never rude, or crude in any way, and in his refined and elegant manner, slowly broke down the walls of the lady's castle and entered with her complete surrender.

In today's world use of Casanova's methods are still valid. Women still love to be pampered, and just seeing a man so concerned about the preparation of the meal, and its presentation is a great foreplay technique in its own right.

Casanova's reputation as one of the world's greatest lovers was built not on secret potions or bedroom tricks, but on the fact that he adored women and devoted himself to them, heart and soul.

Here are some reasons why women loved Casanova as ardently as he loved them.

He thought every woman was special.

No one-to-ten rankings for Casanova. He loved one woman at a time, and although he lavished compliments on them, his praise was based on what made each woman unique. Nothing was too insignificant to mention; he may have admired the way she ate a peach. (When he met Henriette, his greatest love, she was disguised as a soldier; he told her he admired her "whimsical" uniform.) He also liked intelligence and believed that an ugly, witty woman seduced through the charms of her mind. How can you put this lesson into practice? Look for what makes a woman different from everyone else, and tell her how much you appreciate it—one unique comment can be a hundred times more appreciated than a generic "you're so beautiful."

He loved listening to women talk.

Many women read books by or about men to find out what men think, but how many men read books to learn about women? No such fears troubled Casanova. Proud of his masculinity, he would be shocked by anyone who thought it was unmanly to listen to women talk. He once famously said, "I've never made love to a woman whose language I didn't speak because I like to enjoy myself in all my senses at once." In his view, good conversation was the best foreplay—the first step in a seduction—and he liked both partners to take pleasure in it. So instead of taking the conversational lead on your next date, try engaging your date on a topic she's really interested in talking about. You might be surprised by what she has to say.

He treasured and respected women as friends.

Being friends with women was just as important to Casanova as being lovers—he wasn't out to degrade or debauch. He once remarked that women were like books: You need to read more than the title in order to enjoy them. Because of his deep respect for women, he would never "love 'em and leave 'em"—in fact, he maintained close friendships with many of his lovers all his life. It may sound obvious, but treating a potential date with the same attention and respect you'd give to any friend will go a long way toward winning her heart.

He lived life to its fullest.

Casanova felt that happiness was the world's greatest aphrodisiac. He knew that pursuing pleasure and love wasn't a distraction from personal fulfilment, but a worthy end in itself, and he would have laughed at our stressed-out, overachieving culture. To be loved by Casanova was to be well-fed and sensually satiated. Why not take a cue from him? Slow down and celebrate your life. A passion for living is always irresistible. Casanova was a lover of life as well as women.

Casanova is a very different type of lover. A moderately tall (5'9") and comely lad, he was, in his early years, as often the seduced as the seducer. Later in life, he proposed that "when a man is given the time, he achieves his aim by attentiveness, and when he is pressed ... he makes use of presents and gold". He wooed, that is, by kindness and generosity rather than brute force.

He maintained that "four-fifths" of the joy of sex was in giving pleasure to one's partner, and he seems to have had the enviable knack of staying on good terms with many of his former lovers, often for many years.

"You were born to make people happy," wrote one of his "conquests" in a mood of fond nostalgia. What's more, he even practised safe sex, using "a little garment of very fine, transparent skin, eight inches long, closed at one end, but resembling a purse and having at its open end a narrow pink ribbon". And if he is entirely frank about his sexual adventures, he is also fairly brisk and non-salacious - a point which was not always obvious to his earlier readers.

The most popular 19th century edition of the Memoirs was a French version by one Jean Laforgue, who took it upon himself both to suppress parts of the text he didn't like and to turn the author's sprightly original into something at once more pompous and more prurient.

Today, the reader who picks up the Memoirs in search of a bit of pleasing erotica will often be disappointed by the lack of juicy detail: by the standards of modern pornographers, Casanova is a dud.

Once that disappointment is past, though, there are plenty of other attractions on offer. It has been said that the Memoirs offer the fullest and most accurate portrait of 18th century Europe that any single writer ever composed; and also that "no man in history has ... left quite so sincere a record of his life as Casanova".

The adventures are wild enough, but they never read like the self-aggrandising lies of a compulsive braggart. He changed names to protect the prominent, but in other respects this seems to be about as reliable an autobiography as one will ever meet.

A couple of episodes from his childhood may serve to show what an interesting man he was outside the bedroom. The son of professional actors, Casanova was unlucky in losing his father when young, and even more unlucky in his mother, Zanatta, a pretty, snobbish, heartless unintelligent woman with the habit of seeing stupidity almost everywhere save in its true place: herself.

An incident from Giacomo's ninth birthday, on April 2 1734, now seems emblematic. He is being taken by river to Padua, and wakes in the morning to the astonishing sight of trees moving past the portholes. "Mother, what is happening? The trees are walking!"

The adults howl with laughter, and his mother wearily

explains that it is the boat that is moving, not the trees. Giacomo ponders this for a while and then concludes: "So it is possible that the sun does not walk either, but that it is we who move from west to east."

His mother laughs at him, and one of her friends calls him an imbecile. But another adult, a free-thinker called Signor Baffi, tells him that he is quite right, and that from this point on he must never fear to use his reason, no matter how much the crowd may mock.

Another emblem: aged 11, he is brought down to supper for the entertainment of adults. To test the lad's learning and wit, a visiting Englishman writes out a Latin grammarian's riddle for him: "Tell us, grammar experts, why the Latin word for the female organ has the masculine gender, and that for the male has the feminine gender."

Giacomo ponders for a couple of seconds, and then writes out an elegant Latin pentameter: Dice quod a domino nomina servus habet - "Because the slave takes the name of his master".

One does not have to be a card-carrying Freudian to twig that there might be some connection between Casanova's loveless childhood and his tireless search for amorous adventure as a grown man.

The Don Juan type, it has been proposed, is a man whose promiscuity is an endless and doomed hunt for satisfaction in symbolically "conquering" and obliterating a cold mother, via the bodies of unfortunate real-life women.

The Casanova type, while no less insatiable, seeks something much healthier - adult compensation for a boyish lack, with the giving and taking of affection as important a psychological need as repeated orgasms. Casanova had an awful mother as we have seen, vain, snobbish, shallow, utterly self-preoccupied.

On the other hand, somewhere between the zones of "entirely possible" and "all but certain" lies the extraordinary story that one of Mozart's uncredited collaborators on Don Giovanni was none other than Casanova.

You don't need to skim many pages to find that one of the secrets of Casanova's amorous success is that he was, and remains, very good company. Emerson reports "All his life, he struggled to maintain standards of pride, cultural sophistication and dignity that were higher than the society around him. And of course he frequently failed, as often as not betrayed by his own emotions and sensuality. He was a survivor, whose base humanity kept him from ever achieving greatness, but whose spirit links his time with ours more, perhaps, than many of his 'greater' contemporaries."

Chapter 14
The Casanova Complex

Men who have The Casanova Complex find it hard to remain faithful to one woman as they have within patterns of emptiness. The Casanova Complex of having affairs is a form of sexual addiction where a major portion of time the man's time is spent thinking about and pursuing sexual activities. Writer Peter Trachtenburg, who says he has this disorder says, "Any behaviour that is used to anaesthetised pain is likely to become addictive. The need to womanise is a disorder of the feelings characterised by a man's compulsive and addictive-- pursuit and abandonment of women or by symbolic flight through infidelity and multiple relationships."

Men with sexual addictions can be very charming, highly romantic and are masters of instant intimacy. This instant intimacy makes the woman feel special, singled out and valued giving them a rush... The hurry gives the man a relationship rush. The man needs to cement the liaison quickly as he knows that the "bloom" will fade soon. There is emotional fusion due to sharing the erotic excitement and the pseudo-opening of the self.

The man sets up a dependence on the woman for nurture, acceptance and excitement. His relationship with the primary woman (usually his wife) in his life becomes symbiotic. He fears fusion or being sucked into the woman. Affairs are seen as the means of escaping commitment and the sense of being smothered and consumed by the wife. There may be fear of his becoming feminised so he must act out sexually to prove his masculinity. The man flees intimacy and he is frightened of vulnerability. He is afraid of being truly himself with another human being. He is incapable of being himself and has a damaged capacity for connecting on a deep level in a long term relationship. Intimacy feels like being devoured by the woman. He feels invaded, possessed. Normal requests by the woman are seen as demands. The man must withdraw quickly to protect his fragile ego so that he does not get burned, leaving behind a string of broken hearts.

Conclusion

Giacomo Casanova is best known for his prowess in seduction, a master of seduction.... not the perverse kind...a lover that every women coveted over!! Casanova was an extraordinary person, a man of many talents and a man who had many faces. He had a two-faced nature — generous and mean, honest and deceptive, sceptical and gullible, superstitious and rational. He was a man who claimed to have many vocations. He had a passion for a theatrical life. But with all his talents, he frequently succumbed to the quest for pleasure and sex, often avoiding sustained work and established plans, and often got himself into trouble. His true occupation was living largely on his quick wits, steely nerves, luck, social charm, and the money given to him in gratitude and by trickery.

Frequently he ate 50 oysters for breakfast, often with a

companion in his bathtub built for 2. Usually he seduced his friends' wives or daughters, sometimes 2 at a time if we are to believe him. Mostly he played the adventurer: a spy sentenced to jail and escaping over the wall, a lover duelling with an outraged husband, a gambler making several fortunes and spending them on women and wine. Always he lived by his wits.

The incomparable Casanova's guiding philosophy is expressed in a little-quoted passage found midway in his Memoirs: "The instants that man is compelled to give up to misfortune or suffering are so many moments stolen from his life; but he doubles his existence when he has the talent of multiplying his pleasures, no matter of what nature they may be."

The final verdict of the psychoanalyst Lydia Flem is "Beyond pleasure, there is still happiness - such is the insolent legacy of Giacomo Casanova."

Try our hero's techniques, and when you see them working, remember him fondly, as this would have pleased him greatly.

REQUEST FOR FEEDBACK

Dear Reader,

We value your Feedback.

On behalf of the authors we would like to listen to your comments. We are continuously trying to improve the self-help training products created by us to suit the needs of beginners.

Our purpose is to generate **Easy** and **Effective training material** which can cater to the requirements of those who are new to the Pickup Game.

We would request you to give your comments about this

book on its web-page by using the *'Customer Review'* section.

Please tell us what you thought of the product as this will help us and possibly other customers as well. We will apply your suggestions to create improved products in future to suit your particular requirements.

Your Satisfaction is our Inspiration.

Thank you.

Publisher

Casanova Quotes

These quotes are very inspiring and will give you insight into the mind of the Genius.

"As to the deceit perpetrated upon women, let it pass, for, when love is in the way, men and women as a general rule dupe each other."

"By recollecting the pleasures I have had formerly, I renew them, I enjoy them a second time, while I laugh at the remembrance of troubles now past, and which I no longer feel."

"For my future I have no concern, and as a true philosopher, I never would have any, for I know not what it may be: as a Christian, on the other hand, faith must believe without discussion, and the stronger it is, the more it keeps silent."

"God ceases to be God only for those who can admit the possibility of His non-existence, and that conception is in itself the most severe punishment they can suffer."

"God, great principle of all minor principles, God, who is Himself without a principle, could not conceive Himself, if, in order to do it, He required to know His own principle."

"Hatred, in the course of time, kills the unhappy wretch who delights in nursing it in his bosom."

"Heart and head are the constituent parts of character; temperament has almost nothing to do with it, and, therefore, character is dependent upon education, and is susceptible of being corrected and improved."

"I always made my food congenial to my constitution, and my health was always excellent."

"I am bound to add that the excess in too little has ever proved in me more dangerous than the excess in too much; the last may cause indigestion, but the first causes death."

"I don't conquer, I submit."

"I have always loved truth so passionately that I have often resorted to lying as a way of introducing it into the minds which were ignorant of its charms."

"I have felt in my very blood, ever since I was born, a most unconquerable hatred towards the whole tribe of fools, and it arises from the fact that I feel myself a blockhead whenever I am in their company."

"I have had friends who have acted kindly towards me, and it has been my good fortune to have it in my power to give them substantial proofs of my gratitude."

"I have met with some of them - very honest fellows, who, with all their stupidity, had a kind of intelligence and an upright good sense, which cannot be the characteristics of fools."

"I have often met with happiness after some imprudent step which ought to have brought ruin upon me, and although passing a vote of censure upon myself I would thank God for his mercy."

"I know that I have lived because I have felt, and, feeling giving me the knowledge of my existence, I know likewise that I shall exist no more when I shall have ceased to feel."

"I learned very early that our health is always impaired by some excess either of food or abstinence, and I never had any physician except myself."

"I leave to others the decision as to the good or evil tendencies of my character, but such as it is it shines upon my countenance, and there it can easily be detected by any physiognomist."

"I will begin with this confession: whatever I have done in the course of my life, whether it be good or evil, has been done freely; I am a free agent."

"In fact, to gull a fool seems to me an exploit worthy of a witty man."

"In the mean time I worship God, laying every wrong action under an interdict which I endeavour to respect, and I loathe the wicked without doing them any injury."

"It is only necessary to have courage, for strength without self-confidence is useless."

"Love is three quarters curiosity."

"Man is free; yet we must not suppose that he is at liberty to do everything he pleases, for he becomes a slave the moment he allows his actions to be ruled by passion."

"Marriage is the tomb of love."

"My errors will point to thinking men the various roads, and will teach them the great art of treading on the brink of the precipice without falling into it."

"My success and my misfortunes, the bright and the dark days I have gone through, everything has proved to me that in this world, either physical or moral, good comes out of evil just as well as evil comes out of good."

"Real love is the love that sometimes arises after sensual pleasure: if it does, it is immortal; the other kind inevitably goes stale, for it lies in mere fantasy."

"Should I perchance still feel after my death, I would no longer have any doubt, but I would most certainly give the lie to anyone asserting before me that I was dead."

"The history of my life must begin by the earliest circumstance which my memory can evoke; it will therefore commence when I had attained the age of eight years and four months."

"The man who has sufficient power over himself to wait until his nature has recovered its even balance is the truly wise man, but such beings are seldom met with."

"The mind of a human being is formed only of comparisons made in order to examine analogies, and therefore cannot precede the existence of memory."

"The reader of these Memoirs will discover that I never had any fixed aim before my eyes, and that my system, if it can be called a system, has been to glide away unconcernedly on the stream of life, trusting to the wind wherever it led."

"Thence, I suppose, my natural disposition to make fresh acquaintances, and to break with them so readily, although always for a good reason, and never through mere fickleness."

"We avenge intellect when we dupe a fool, and it is a victory not to be despised for a fool is covered with steel and it is often very hard to find his vulnerable part."

"Worthy or not, my life is my subject, and my subject is my life."

"You will be amused when you see that I have more than once deceived without the slightest qualm of conscience, both knaves and fools."

Made in the USA
Lexington, KY
08 June 2010